Run

A DEVOTIONAL
ON THE LIFE
OF JONAH

Chad Stafford

Grace Lake
PUBLISHING

Run: A Devotional on the Life of Jonah
ISBN: 979-8-9866215-4-8
Publisher: INICIO by Grace Lake Publishing (June 23, 2023)
Cover design by: Brandon Baker
Formatting and Layout by: Virginia Mathers
Printed in the United States of America

DEDICATION

I'd like to dedicate this book to my parents,
Charlie and Sharon Stafford.

When the child of Christ-honoring parents runs
from God, it must be a pain they find excruciating.
I don't know how my parents stayed firm and yet filled
with grace for their Jonah (me).

If my parents would have given me any reason to keep
running from God, I would have stayed away forever. They
were consistent with their discipline and spoke faith over me
whether I wanted to hear it or not.

They modeled this scripture before me
which ultimately made the gospel irresistible:

**"Therefore, my beloved brothers, be steadfast,
immovable, always abounding in the work of the Lord,
knowing that in the Lord your labor is not in vain."**
1 CORINTHIANS 15:58, NIV

Thanks, Mom and Dad.
I love you so much,
Bub

Day 1

**"The word of the Lord came
to Jonah son of Amittai."**
JONAH 1:1

Most of us have been at events where the keynote speaker has been introduced in this way: "Our guest tonight certainly needs no introduction." This applies to the main character of the book of Jonah: Jonah the prophet.

Typically, when we read the Bible and a character is introduced, we learn something about their background. In the book of Jonah, no background is given. This leads us to ask the question: why? The conclusion is that Jonah has no introduction because, in his day, Jonah needed no introduction. His reputation preceded him.

The book of 2 Kings tells us that Jonah ministered during the reign of King Jeroboam II who reigned from 786 BC - 746 BC. But it also gives us incredible insight into Jonah and his character.

**"In the fifteenth year of Amaziah son of Joash king
of Judah, Jeroboam son of Jehoash king of Israel
became king in Samaria, and he reigned forty-one
years. He did evil in the eyes of the Lord and did not
turn away from any of the sins of Jeroboam son
of Nebat, which he had caused Israel to commit.
He was the one who restored the boundaries
of Israel from Lebo Hamath to the Dead Sea,
in accordance with the word of the Lord, the God**

**of Israel, spoken through his servant Jonah
son of Amittai, the prophet from Gath Hepher."**
2 KINGS 14:23-25

The other prophets God used during this time were Amos and Hosea. These prophets criticized King Jeroboam for his injustice and unfaithfulness, and for his aggressive military policy to extend Israel's power and influence.

Jonah did not criticize him; he actually endorsed the king's actions. He liked how King Jeroboam handled issues. The people of Jonah's day knew him as highly patriotic and a highly partisan nationalist. And every one of them would have been floored by what God asked Jonah to do next.

Jonah's reputation had preceded him, and God was wanting him to be delivered from his pride so that He could use him in a new way.

TODAY'S PRAYER
**Father, please be bigger in my life than my pride,
my ego, my opinions, and my reputation. Do a new
work in me and through me. Let me be known
for my faithfulness to You and Your Word.**

■　■　■

Day 2

**"Go to the great city of Nineveh and
preach against it, because its wickedness
has come up before me."**
JONAH 1:1-2

Before we get too judgmental about Jonah and his reluctance
to go to Nineveh, we need to put ourselves in his shoes. God
commanded a man to preach to the very people that he feared
most and hated like poison.

What God told Jonah to do was unprecedented. Until this
point, God's prophets had only been sent to God's people,
the Hebrews.

Assyria was not only not Jewish; but they were also one of the
cruelest, most violent empires of ancient history. They would
torture, dismember, and decapitate their enemies in a truly
barbaric fashion. They would typically cut off their legs and
one arm, and leave one arm and hand attached so they could
mockingly shake their hand as they died. They would make
their enemies' friends and family members parade with their
loved ones' heads elevated on poles. The Assyrians have been
called a terrorist state.

Nothing about this mission made any sense.

Why would God ask anyone to betray his country's interests
like this? How could a good God give a nation like Assyria even
the slightest chance to experience His mercy? Why on Earth
would God be helping the enemy of His people?

God would never send a warning unless there was a chance that judgment could have been averted, and Jonah knew that very well. Jonah, however, didn't just have a problem with the job he was given; he had a bigger problem with the One who gave it to him. Jonah doubted the goodness, wisdom, and justice of God. He didn't think that God knew what He was doing.

Today, we have the benefit of seeing that God is not just sending Jonah there solely to deliver a wicked people from His wrath. God is sending Jonah to Nineveh to deliver Jonah. He is wanting to change Jonah's thinking, his worldview, and his entire concept of God. God is wanting Jonah to see Nineveh through His eyes.

God didn't see Nineveh as hopeless or worthless. God didn't call them the reprobate city, He called them "the great city." God wants to become bigger in Jonah's life, and it's going to be Jonah's decision whether he is going to allow it to happen.

TODAY'S PRAYER
Father, may I open my heart to You and allow You to become bigger in my life. Deliver me from my pride, my prejudices, and my narrow views. Help me to hear Your voice and see with Your eyes today.

■　■　■

Day 3

"Go to the great city of Nineveh and preach against it, because its wickedness has come up before me."
JONAH 1:1-2

God talked to Jonah like an army general to a soldier: "This plan looks suicidal, but it's gonna work."

Which begs the question for us as followers of Jesus: what do we do with what we perceive as difficult orders from God? Especially when we fail to see the logic. An old preacher once said to me, "Son, when we can't see God's hand, it's then that we learn to trust God's heart." In turbulent times, and during times of battle, we must take comfort in the qualifications of the General. I obey my orders and go. When God gives us seemingly crazy directions, it's up to us to move and take refuge in His record.

For those of us who struggle with trust, maybe because of an abusive situation we have been in with our parents or other relationships, this is a muscle that we must develop in our walk with God. It is not easy, but it is vital to our spiritual development.

One way we can begin to grow in our trust is by realizing that there is a major difference between pain and harm. If the doctor has to do surgery to remove cancer, there will be pain after it. We will be sore for a little while, but we will recover. Although it might have been painful, the goal of the surgery was to heal us and remove harm from us. Pain is not harmful.

When God leads us through painful seasons, we develop trust by saying to ourselves: this situation hurts, but I know that God is not trying to harm me.

We should also learn to develop trust with our brothers and sisters in Christ. When someone that we love and who has proven themselves repeatedly in showing that they love us and support us, has a painful conversation with us about something in our lives that concerns them, we cannot immediately jump to the assumption that they are trying to harm us.

It may be painful to hear, but we need to ask ourselves a few questions so that we can grow and have the proper perspective.
1. What is their track record?
2. Have they served us?
3. Have they been good to us?
4. Have they made significant deposits into our lives?

God works with authority, not around it. God did not send Jonah to Nineveh to harm him; He sent him to Nineveh to heal him and to save them. God not only sent us His Word to heal and save us, but He also sent us brothers and sisters in Christ.

God often heals His family, through His family.

TODAY'S PRAYER
Father, help me to grow in my trust in You and in the people that You have sent into my life. You want to bless me and not harm me. I want to walk in Your blessings for my life and I realize that growing in my trust is key to this. I choose to begin this today.

■ ■ ■

Day 4

**"But Jonah ran away from the Lord
and headed for Tarshish."**
JONAH 1:3(A)

God told Jonah to go east, and he went west in the exact opposite direction. Jonah tried to run to Tarshish because it was believed to be the outermost western rim of the world known to Israel at the time.

Jonah refused to go. He didn't like the people and he wanted them to get everything that was coming to them. He refused to go preach repentance and God's mercy and grace to them. The reason why Jonah couldn't preach grace, repentance, and mercy was that he was a stranger to it himself.

The gospel teaches us that all people are completely fallen from God, and only by His mercy and grace can we come to Him and be welcomed into His family. When we know this, we can never feel superior to anyone.

Jonah's pride in his own national pedigree made him cowardly. Our pride destroys God's grace. Our pride keeps us confused because we feel superior to people. We can never be effective when we have an inflated view of ourselves. But if we humble ourselves and see God's grace for what it is, we can never feel superior to anyone, because we know that we didn't deserve His grace either. We echo the words of the Apostle Paul in **EPHESIANS 2:1-5** who said, **"We were dead in our sins but God who is rich in mercy, has brought us back to life again."** In the book of Leviticus, God tells His people how to live the best possible life. He instructs them how to live with integrity, righteousness, and generosity.

One example of this is when He tells them to not harvest the edges of their fields but to "leave the edges for the widow, the orphan, and the stranger in the midst (foreigner)." God wanted to provide for the most vulnerable people in their society in a way that would not rob them of any dignity.

And with every direction God gives to them, He tells them why. "Because you were slaves in Egypt and I delivered you." In other words, God was saying, "You were the most vulnerable people in the world once too. You didn't deserve it either, but I took care of you. Don't forget where you came from. Be kind and gentle to them because I was kind and gentle to you."

Pride blocks the grace of God and only creates more darkness in a world already void of light. But when we open our hearts to God's grace, our hearts not only get bigger but so does our world.

TODAY'S PRAYER
Father, I thank you today for your incredible grace to me. Help me to be quick to extend it to everyone around me, because "I was once a slave in Egypt and You delivered me."

■ ■ ■

Day 5

"He went down to Joppa, where he found a ship bound for that port. After paying the fare, he went aboard and sailed for Tarshish to flee from the Lord."
JONAH 1:3

God told Jonah to go east, and he went west. He told him to go by land, and he went by sea.

He was sent to the big city of Nineveh, and instead he bought a one-way ticket to the end of the world.

This passage shows us that if we want to run from God, there will always be a ship willing to take us.

If we want to cheat on our diet, there will always be an occasion to do it.

If we harbor lustful thoughts, there will eventually be a bed.

If we are easily offended, opportunities to be offended will come at us nonstop.

If we want to relapse and go back to alcoholism and drug use, Satan will always provide a reason and an opportunity for that to happen.

Our jobs will start to stress us out.

Our relationships and friendships will take a turn for the worse, and we will begin to feel lonely.

Our marriage will start to have some problems, or some tragedy will strike, and all we want is to have some momentary relief.

If we live life on the short term, we will always look to do the easy thing and run. But while we are running, we need to understand that there is no refuge *from* God; there is only refuge *in* God.

Jonah served God; but when Jonah's test came, he froze. The things that he believed and was familiar with, were of no help to him. He had never experienced the reality of the grace of God personally and as a result, he failed badly.

Sometimes life hurts and it continues to hurt because our fingers are in the doorway of a door that God keeps trying to close. When we continue doing things our way, we pay a heavy price for it. But if we humble ourselves and give God the rightful place in our lives, we see that He actually works with us, not against us.

The essence of sin is running from God. The first step in following Jesus is declaring that "I am a fugitive and on the run from God."

TODAY'S PRAYER
Father, I choose today to obey You. Life is too hard without You to do things on my own and too awesome with You to even try.

■　■　■

Day 6

**"Then the Lord sent a great wind on the sea,
and such a violent storm arose that the ship
threatened to break up."**
JONAH 1:4

Jonah was called to do something. Jonah ran from it and God pursued him. And how did God pursue him? He sent a storm.

Jonah ran, but God would not let him go. Isn't that good to know? That even when we run from God, He runs toward us.

In my opinion, the phrase "God sent a great wind" does not do the text enough justice. The King James Version says, "God hurled a great wind upon the sea."

The word "hurled" is often used for throwing a weapon, like a spear. The Gulf Coast interpretation of this phrase is, "God threw down on Jonah."

Why is this important? The good and bad news of living in the world as a Child of God is this: There will always be a storm attached to our sin.

The DUI that we may have gotten was a loving storm to open our eyes to the fact that our drinking had gotten out of control, and we could have killed an innocent person.

The pornography that has been exposed was a love note from God that our eyes have not been guarded, and that we are putting things in our hearts that will cause an affair, affecting our kids down through future generations.

The debt collector calling us may be an alert from Jesus exposing that our spending habits are out of control. And we are one weak moment away from stealing from our employers and going to jail for embezzlement.

Visiting the casino and losing a ton of money is a wonderful alarm clock from God trying to open our eyes to the fact that we are living with an out-of-control desire for more. We need to get on a budget and learn how to create financial margin.

The market drying up in our field of business may be God showing us that we have got to get off the hamster wheel of buy, sell, and cover. We should no longer "borrow from Peter to pay Paul," but begin pouring our resources into a new area that is going to produce for years to come.

In the middle of the storm, there is loving attention. When God shows us how weak we are, the storms are reminders of His grace before we come to the end of our lives without Him.

The real person of Jesus was thrown into the storm of God's wrath. And because of that sacrifice, God's wrath has subsided.

> **"As Jonah was assigned to the Ninevites so**
> **the son of man is assigned to this generation."**
> **MATTHEW 12:40**

During a storm, we learn to trust God. He uses gentle power and tender violence, and that is what the grace of God is. We can conclude that God loves us by the fact that He chases after us. He continues to pursue us.

Grace is fierce, dogged, and determined love. It won't stop pursuing us and will hurt us just enough to wake us up.

TODAY'S PRAYER

**Father, help me today to walk in obedience
and wisdom. I don't want to have to go through
a self-inflicted storm for You to get my attention.
My mind is alert, and my heart is receptive.
You are the Lord of my life and where You lead,
I will follow.**

■ ■ ■

Day 7

"Then the Lord sent a great wind on the sea, and such a violent storm arose that the ship threatened to break up. All the sailors were afraid and each cried out to his own god. And they threw the cargo into the sea to lighten the ship."
JONAH 1:4-5

No matter who we are, we all cry out to God in extreme conditions. Our spiritual life may be beneath the surface very deep, but extreme conditions always bring it out. The storms of life help us see how much we need God.

The prayer of terror, however, is not a sign of God's grace working in our hearts. The prayer of terror is a natural response of the heart to extreme conditions. The Apostle Paul knew this and wrote about it in his letter to the Romans.

"The wrath of God is being revealed from heaven against all the godlessness and wickedness of people, who suppress the truth by their wickedness."
ROMANS 1:18

Paul said that every human being intuitively knows that God exists. All of us deep down have the truth of the knowledge of God in our hearts and just won't admit it. He knows this because we were made in God's divine image. At some deep level, even the fiercest skeptic knows there is a God.

When it comes to the truth of God, Paul said, not only does everyone have it, but we are all suppressing it. The word "suppress" means to prevent someone from exercising power. To suppress the truth means that we hold it under the water and drown it.

We do this by trying to smother our first-order belief, "I know there is a God," with a second-order belief, "I believe in a god who lets me live however I want." *That* is suppression.

When it comes to truth, it's not that God hasn't spoken; it's that we are not obeying. We often deny the truth because we refuse to deal with reality. We bargain with God instead of trusting and surrendering because we don't believe that He loves us.

If the only time we call out to God is when we are in trouble, God doesn't consider that worship. He sees it for what it truly is: desperation. We know that God wants to rule our hearts. We still want to be in charge. And until we submit to Him, we are just clinging to something that is a false god.

The true sign of worship is surrender.

TODAY'S PRAYER
Father, today I submit my life to You. I hold nothing back. May my life be a daily act of worship where I surrender and trust You.

■ ■ ■

Day 8

"But Jonah had gone below deck, where he lay down and fell into a deep sleep."
JONAH 1:6(A)

The nineteenth-century Scottish minister Hugh Martin states that Jonah was sleeping "the sleep of sorrow."

Many of us know that desire to escape reality through sleep, even for a little while. Jonah was spent, exhausted, and drained by anger, guilt, anxiety, and grief.

Dr. David Guzik makes an incredible observation here about Jonah sleeping below deck when he writes the following passage:

The nature of Jonah's sleep is also instructive, and too much like the sleep of the careless Christian: Jonah slept in a place where he hoped no one would see him or disturb him. "Sleeping Christians" like to "hide out" among the church. Jonah slept in a place where he could not help with the work that needed to be done. "Sleeping Christians" stay away from the work of the Lord.

Jonah slept while there was a prayer meeting up on the deck. "Sleeping Christians" don't like prayer meetings.

Jonah slept and had no idea of the problems around him.

"Sleeping Christians" don't know what is really going on. Jonah slept when he was in great danger. "Sleeping Christians" are in danger, but don't know it.

Jonah slept while the heathen needed him. "Sleeping Christians" snooze on while the world needs their message and testimony.

Some sleeping Christians protest that they are not asleep at all.

"We talk about Jesus" — but you can talk in your sleep.

"We have a walk for Jesus" — but you can walk in your sleep.

"We have passion for Jesus — I just wept in worship the other day" - but you can cry in your sleep.

"We have joy and rejoice in Jesus" — but you can laugh in your sleep.

"We think about Jesus all the time" — but you can think while you are asleep; we call it dreaming.

Guzik, D. (n.d.). *Jonah 1 - Jonah Runs from God*. Enduring Word Bible Commentary. Retrieved May 11, 2023 from https://enduringword.com/bible-commentary/jonah-1/

TODAY'S PRAYER
Father, help me wake up and see the needs that are all around me. Help me to be active with my faith. Keep me ever mindful that You want to work in my life even in the middle of a storm.

■　■　■

Day 9

"The captain went to him and said, 'How can you sleep? Get up and call on your god. Maybe he will take notice of us so that we will not perish.'"
JONAH 1:6(B)

Jonah was asleep below deck while everyone upstairs was praying and fighting against the storm. He might have been out of touch with his situation, but the captain is extremely alert. Jonah was thoroughly absorbed by his own problems, but the captain was seeking the common good of everyone in the boat.

As believers, we are called to take our faith and use it for the public good. Everyone on the boat was praying to their own god, but Jonah did not pray to his. The captain rebuked Jonah for not doing this. Jonah was so wrapped up in his own problems that he slept. He was full of his own grief and self-doubt. He was completely distant from the problems of everyone around him and did not use his faith to help them.

The secular world has every right to evaluate us on what we do for our community. Jonah deserved to be rebuked, and churches that don't seek the common good for their society deserve to be rebuked, too. The same storm that threatens one person threatens all of us. The safety of everyone depends on each of us. Jonah ran because he didn't want to work for the good of pagans; he only cared about fellow believers. As followers of Jesus, we are not only part of a faith community; we are part of the human community. Everyone who has ever been born was made in the image of God; therefore, everyone matters to God.

The two biggest problems of the church world are not knowing about the world's problems or knowing about them and choosing to not do anything about them. God doesn't want us to be asleep to the issues outside. The world is watching and waiting and needing our help.

Everyone's life is at stake. Our healing is bigger than us. It's about the greater good of our society as well. We begin to see that, once we get up and start moving.

To us, Jonah represents the church before a watching world, one where God wakes us up and helps us to realize that we are capable of changing things.

TODAY'S PRAYER
Father, Your world needs fearless Christians who understand the times they live in. Help me choose to use my faith to make a difference in my home, on my job, in my church, and in my community.

■　■　■

Day 10

"Then the sailors said to each other, 'Come, let us cast lots to find out who is responsible for this calamity.' They cast lots and the lot fell on Jonah. So they asked him, 'Tell us, who is responsible for making all this trouble for us? What kind of work do you do? Where do you come from? What is your country? From what people are you?'"
JONAH 1:7-8

Because of the intensity behind it, the sailors were spiritually aware enough to sense that this was not just a random storm. It came out of nowhere and had a sense of judgment on it. They concluded that somebody had sinned.

We can take notice of the nature of their questions and see some incredible insight here. "What kind of work do you do? Who are your people? Where do you come from?" The sailors were asking Jonah identity questions.

Who we are and who we worship is the most foundational layer of our identity. Everyone gets their identity from something. The sailors knew that our identity is rooted in the things we give allegiance to and things we look to save us.

The sailors' goal in asking Jonah these questions wasn't to get to know him. They wanted to know why God was mad at him. The sailors were not in the least bit narrow-minded and bigoted like Jonah. They were open to calling on Jonah's God. In fact, they were more ready to do this than he was.

But Jonah's identity was shallow. A shallow identity prevents us from seeing ourselves in the right way and creates hostility toward people who are different from us. Jonah didn't like people who weren't like him and who didn't worship like him. Without the power of God's grace, he will be unable to change, and so will we.

Can't you see the irony here? God is not some vigilante. He is a master teacher. Jonah didn't believe that God could change Nineveh nor did he even want to. He was proud and scared at the same time.

How do we look at our society? Do we believe that radical change is possible? We must want our communities to be changed. Are we intimidated by it? Do we believe that we can really make a difference in their lives?

There are many church attendees who, just like Jonah, don't even care about their city and the people who are in the boat with them. While we live, we are here for the common good of our world and to introduce to them the love of their Heavenly Father. God used the sailors to remind Jonah of that; however, Jonah was proud and cynical all at the same time. Until Jonah was willing to die to himself, he was of no good to them. The same goes for followers of Jesus.

TODAY'S PRAYER
Father, today help me remember that my life is not about me. It's about You and it's about others. I am important, but I am not the most important. May my identity be built on You and Your word.

■ ■ ■

Day 11

**"He answered, 'I am a Hebrew and I worship
the Lord, the God of heaven, who made the sea and
the dry land.' This terrified them and they asked,
'What have you done?'"**
*(They knew he was running away from the Lord
because he had already told them so.)*
**The sea was getting rougher and rougher.
So they asked him, 'What should we do to you
to make the sea calm down for us?' 'Pick me up
and throw me into the sea,' he replied, 'and it will
become calm. I know that it is my fault that this
great storm has come upon you.'"**
JONAH 1:9-12

The great theologians are divided as to why Jonah was doing this. Fifty percent think that Jonah was humbling himself before God and repenting. Jonah was saying "God, I was wrong, please forgive me."

The other fifty percent of theologians think it was rebellion, not repentance. They feel that Jonah was saying, "I'd rather die than go to Nineveh. Just kill me." It might not have been repentance, just pity. At least, he was finally taking responsibility.

Jonah's journey away from his pride and self-righteousness will be a slow one, as we will see throughout this series. In today's devotion we are going to examine this passage from the angle of repentance, because if it is, there are some wonderful things we can learn.

Up until this point, Jonah had resisted doing anything or even talking to the sailors. For the first time, Jonah stopped talking about his problems and talking about himself and started talking about God. Jonah quoted God's greatness. **"I am a Hebrew and I worship the Lord, the God of heaven, who made the sea and the dry land."**

If he was repenting, Jonah was saying, "How could I be doing this? I was so stupid to think I could get away with this. I was so ungrateful to the One who gave me every aspect of my being." Jonah says, "I am a Hebrew. My people were enslaved, and I was removed from captivity so that I could represent God to the world, and I have hidden that with my actions."

Jonah was finally getting his mind off himself. What a gift. What a blessing. True repentance is getting our minds to start thinking about the bigger picture; off of ourselves and our problems. He doesn't talk about himself that much and real repentance does that.

True repentance is *realizing* that our problems, our goals, our hurt feelings, and our agendas are not the *main* thing.

Jonah's repentance was different from what we see with the sailors who were looking to find out the reason, the cause, and the blame. The sailors were obsessed with one thing: "How do I get out of this mess?" Their question was, "What should we do to make the seas calm down *for us?*"

The sailors were willing to go to God because they were willing to do anything to get out of their situation. True repentance is not worrying about ourselves or how to get out of our messes.

Jonah owned his mess and said, "You guys are dying for me, but I should be dying for you. Throw me in." When we repent, we don't demand our rights; we let God call the shots. That repentance leads to freedom.

Jonah stopped defending himself and, when he did, he began thinking right and he had courage. Jonah realized that his storm and sin were affecting everyone on the boat and everyone else on a boat nearby.

Someone else's sin may have profoundly affected us, but the same storm that is out to get me is also going to get others. And unless we take responsibility and own it, everybody will drown.

TODAY'S PRAYER
Father, help me keep You as the main focus of my life. May You become so big that the other things remain small.

■　■　■

Day 12

"He answered, 'I am a Hebrew and I worship
the Lord, the God of heaven, who made the sea and
the dry land.' This terrified them and they asked,
'What have you done?'
*(They knew he was running away from the Lord
because he had already told them so.)*
The sea was getting rougher and rougher. So they
asked him, 'What should we do to you to make the
sea calm down for us?' 'Pick me up and throw me
into the sea,' he replied, 'and it will become calm.
I know that it is my fault that this great storm has
come upon you.' Instead, the men did their best to
row back to land. But they could not, for the sea
grew even wilder than before. Then they cried out to
the Lord, 'Please, Lord, do not let us die for taking
this man's life. Do not hold us accountable for
killing an innocent man, for you, Lord, have done as
you pleased.' Then they took Jonah and threw him
overboard, and the raging sea grew calm."

JONAH 1:9-15

As mentioned yesterday, the great theologians are divided as to why Jonah is asking to be thrown overboard. Fifty percent think that Jonah was humbling himself before God and repenting. Jonah was saying "God, I was wrong, please forgive me."

The other fifty percent of theologians think it was rebellion. They feel that Jonah was saying, "I'd rather die than go to Nineveh. Just kill me."

Either way, he was finally taking responsibility.

Examining this passage from the angle of repentance can teach some wonderful things about God's grace and patience.

When God shows us how weak we are, that reminds us of His grace before we come to the end of our lives without Him. The only way we will drown is by continually running from His grace. Jonah realized this, and when he got thrown in, what did he find? Love beneath the waves.

In the middle of the storms of our lives, we can see God's loving attention. Jonah saw this and was thrown into the middle of it, and he trusted God.

Jonah realized that the surefire way of drowning was to keep running from God, so he allowed himself to be hurled into it. As he did, for the first time in his life, Jonah didn't just know doctrines about God; he knew God himself, personally.

When we obey God in dark times, we find gracious provision. God continues to show us that the way up is down, and the only way to rule is to submit. When we give up pursuing our own happiness and give ourselves to God, we find joy.

God sends storms to show us *who we are*. We get to choose who we are going to be. We can be angry and run through life feeling like we deserve better, or we can humble ourselves and he can lift us up higher and higher.

Jonah ran because he wanted to get away from the heathens, and he found himself surrounded by them, ultimately giving his life for them.

God called Jonah to do something that He knew Jonah would fail at. He did this to show him the major flaws inside his own soul. God knew that Jonah would not be competent to preach until he failed and fell flat on his face, and God does the same thing to us.

Continual success creates a shallowness in our character. As we examine history, we see that great leaders are ones who faced terrible failures and frustrations. The storms don't make us better; it's how we respond to them that creates depth and wisdom. They don't automatically turn us into a wise and deep person. Storms will either devastate us or deepen us; it is our choice.

TODAY'S PRAYER
Father, help me keep You as the main focus of my life. May You become so big that the other things remain small.

■　■　■

Day 13

**"And the Lord appointed a great fish to swallow up
Jonah. And Jonah was in the belly of the fish
three days and three nights."**
JONAH 1:17 (ESV)

Running to the sea meant Jonah chose chaos and separation
over obedience. For ancient Israel, the sea was a metaphor for
chaos and evil. The Hebrews were not a seafaring people. They
were comfortable sticking close to the coast and to the Sea
of Galilee.

Throughout the prophets, the enemies of God and His people
rose up out of the sea. Jonah chose that chaos and uncertainty
over the peace and order that comes from submitting to God.

Many of us do the same. We would rather have the chaos of self-
reliance and indulgence, than the security of submission and
restraint. Restrained people are rarely chaotic people.

Is your life peaceful or chaotic? Your finances? Your
relationships? Your home?

God desires to bring wholeness to our chaos. He's been doing
that since the beginning. But there are times when God uses
chaos to get us to wholeness.

God led the fish to Jonah. Even in his defiance and rebellion,
Jonah can't avoid God's power. By causing the storm and
sending the fish, God demonstrated that there is no amount
of chaos, brokenness, heartbreak, rejection, or sin outside

of His intervention. Even the strongest forces of nature and supernatural power still have to submit to Him.

TODAY'S PRAYER

God, thank you for bringing peace to the chaotic parts of my life. Thank you for also using those chaotic areas to display your power and grace in my life. I praise you, because you work in and through all of it to draw me closer and make you more like you.

■ ■ ■

Day 14

**"Then Jonah prayed to the Lord his God from
the belly of the fish, saying, 'I called out to the Lord,
out of my distress, and he answered me; out of the
belly of Sheol I cried, and you heard my voice.'"**
JONAH 2:1–2 (ESV)

From the belly of the fish, out of distress, out of the belly of
Sheol. Three places where people might think God's not going
to hear you.

One of the biggest reasons we don't think God is listening is
shame. We do not feel worthy enough or good enough to talk
to God. "God would never want to deal with me; I've done too
much and gone too far." Few things cripple us more than shame.
It is paralyzing to deal with the feelings of worthlessness and
helplessness. We recognize our sin and buy in to the lie that we
are disqualified from God's love.

Another reason? Embarrassment. "What if people know? What
if they all find out?" One of the things about embarrassment
is that it assumes people don't know how messed up we are or
that they're not messed up either. News flash — we're all pretty
messed up! Avoiding reaching out to God because we're too
embarrassed is like not admitting to your doctor you don't eat
well. He already knows. Quit assuming that people who already
don't like you will care; the people who love you won't care.

A final reason is pride. We think we're too good to humble
ourselves before God and admit our struggle. If shame is
thinking we're not good enough, then pride is thinking we're

too good. Pride elevates us higher than reality would allow, and it places us at the center of our existence. Pride is its own form of idolatry.

Most of us will never find ourselves at the world's end, buried in the belly of a whale, but we've all been too ashamed to admit we need help. We've all allowed embarrassment to keep us stuck in distress, not asking for prayer or asking for forgiveness. Many of us have been too proud to admit it feels we're going through Hades itself; that we're walking around in torment and fear, a living hell.

God wants you at this moment. You don't have to have it all together, all figured out. Cry out, wherever you are, and He will hear you.

TODAY'S PRAYER
Lord, forgive me for allowing shame, embarrassment, and pride from coming to You in prayer, asking for Your help. Thank You for being quick to listen to my cries for help.

■　■　■

Day 15

"For you cast me into the deep, into the heart of the seas, and the flood surrounded me; all your waves and your billows passed over me."
JONAH 2:3 (ESV)

There is no hope on the run. Notice Jonah's language here. It carried a huge tone of desperation and fatigue.

Running from God is exhausting. We hide from friends, from family, and from our church that loves us. One of the devil's most powerful tools is keeping us on the run in shame, embarrassment, and pride.

Sin and brokenness will eventually overcome our lives and saturate our perspective. We understand the words of David when he said, "My sin is ever before me."

So often, running from God is our first instinct in moments of fear or failure. But if we give ourselves a moment to pause, we can see that it is counterintuitive. Why do we run from the only One who can help us? Like a wounded animal, we bite and lash out at the very hand trying to free us.

Again, we see God's control over the chaos. The waves and billows of water are from God. The heart of the sea and the deep are at the control of the power of God.

All too often, we make the mistake of assuming that God is detached from our chaos, that He is repelled or resisted by it.

God is over it as He is all things, sovereign and compassionate, and ready to turn it for His benefit and our good.

TODAY'S PRAYER
God, thank You for Your sovereignty. Thank You that when I can't seem to trace You, I can trust You. Your power over the chaos of my life is more than enough to see me through. I stop running from You today, and I yield myself to Your Lordship. Call the shots, and I will be quick to listen and obey.

■   ■   ■

Day 16

**"Then I said, 'I am driven away from your sight;
yet I shall again look upon your holy temple.
The waters closed in over me to take my life; the
deep surrounded me; weeds were wrapped about
my head at the roots of the mountains. I went down
to the land whose bars closed upon me forever;
yet you brought up my life from the pit,
O Lord my God.'"**
JONAH 2:4–6 (ESV)

No matter how far you run, you're never too far from God.

We are entering into the crux of the passage. This is the moment when Jonah's attitude began to change, and the sliver of hope began to grow. He talked about being driven away (even though he was the one who ran), and *yet* he knew he would see the temple again.

He used the language of drowning, of being pulled down to a watery grave at the roots of the mountain. He was being sent to the land whose gates are eternally closed, and *yet* God brought him back up.

The two *yets*...both are true. We do feel driven from God's sight, we do experience the suffocating entrapment of our own sin and darkness. We feel as though all is lost and over with; that the only outcome of our sin will be a spiritual defeat.

But we must hold on to words like *yet*. The Bible is full of these turning point moments. The *yets*, the howevers, and the nevertheless. These are the moments where God does the impossible and defies the inevitable.

Jonah saw himself completely separated from the light of God's presence and was concerned that he would never see hope again. He found something to hold on to, something to endure. He knew that God could *yet* restore him.

We are reminded of **ACTS 17:27** where Paul said to the philosophers of Athens, **"that they should seek God, and perhaps feel their way toward him and find him. Yet he is actually not far from each one of us."**

Or the writer of Hebrews, encouraging us that **"without faith it is impossible to please him, for whoever would draw near to God must believe that he exists and that he rewards those who seek him." - HEBREWS 11:6 (ESV)**

God sees us all, and anyone who turns to see Him will always find Him. We deceive ourselves into thinking we are far from God, when, He is only one step away.

TODAY'S PRAYER
Thank You, God, that You write the "yets"
in our story. We allow sin and disobedience to drive us
away from You, YET You are still faithful. Faithful
to love us, faithful to draw us, faithful to forgive us.
We seek You today knowing that You are
ever-present and willing to help us.

■ ■ ■

Day 17

**"When my life was fainting away,
I remembered the Lord, and my prayer
came to you, into your holy temple."**
JONAH 2:7 (ESV)

Restoration starts with remembering.

We must remember that our prayers always reach God. While Daniel spoke of prayers being hindered (**DANIEL 10**), that's only one passage in the light of countless others testifying to the fact that God hears the cries of His people.

If you have followed God for a few days, a few years, or most of your life, you can remember a moment when He was close. It may be a moment of prayer, a moment of service, or a moment of worship. Whatever it is, you can testify to the goodness of God.

For Jonah, to remember didn't imply that he forgot. It meant that he recalled his God, that he reminded himself, and declared who God was. Perhaps in your fading faith, you simply need to say one thing out loud that demonstrates God's goodness to you. Recount a moment of His faithfulness. Reminisce on provision, healing, or encouragement He brought you.

That prayer of remembrance and declaration will find its way to God. Jonah had artistically painted the image of total separation and darkness; and yet, in a fleeting few seconds of hopelessness and despair, Jonah spoke of YHWH, his faithful, powerful, loving, benevolent, creating, redeeming, restoring, providing, present God. That prayer brought him to life. It restored and renewed his soul. His faith blossomed and his hope was strengthened.

Take time to remember. You may feel discouraged or down, separated, and isolated, but you can find a moment when the goodness of God was present in your life. You can use that ember to spark renewal.

TODAY'S PRAYER
Today, Father, I recall Your goodness to me.
Thank You for Your faithfulness, Your steadfast love, and Your devotion to Your covenant with me. You are such a good Father. Help me to always remember all Your benefits when I am down or discouraged.

■ ■ ■

Day 18

**"But I with the voice of thanksgiving
will sacrifice to you; what I have vowed I will pay.
Salvation belongs to the Lord!"**
JONAH 2:9 (ESV)

Only God can save. No matter what situation he found himself in, Jonah remembered that YHWH, the Lord, was his only hope of salvation.

It's an idea that's easy to forget.

In our distress or panic, we look to so many other things to save us such as money, relationships, possessions, or our jobs. The irony of this is that we look to some of the very things that distract us from God to save us. Other prophets like Isaiah pointed out the futility of worshiping things that are created just like us, or even things that we created (**ISAIAH 44**). Why do we pursue money? Power? Influence? All of these are temporary and can be taken away or lost in a moment. Only God is truly eternal; so therefore, He is the only logical One to save us.

At some point, Jonah lost sight of this. He thought that he could outrun God's plan for him, but in doing so, he ran right into it. He needed the very salvation he was being called to proclaim. He found himself in the exact spiritual position as the people of Nineveh. Lost and separated, Jonah felt he was doomed to destruction. And he found the same salvation they required.

But the point that Jonah made here is critical: "Salvation belongs to YHWH!" He recovered his trust and belief that his

God, the God of his people was his only hope of salvation.

> **"And the Lord spoke to the fish, and it vomited
> Jonah out upon the dry land."**
> **JONAH 2:10 (ESV)**

Not every restoration is beautiful, and not every redemption is painless. But better to be out of sin and covered in vomit than stuck in the belly of judgment.

TODAY'S PRAYER
God, thank You for the sacrifice of Your son Jesus. Because of His sacrifice, I have access to You. You are my only hope of salvation. You are my deliverance. You are my peace. When I run, Your Holy Spirit still pursues me. Help me to continue to obey Your instructions so that I may live in relationship with You every day.

■ ■ ■

Day 19

"Then the word of the Lord came to Jonah a second time: 'Go to the great city of Nineveh and proclaim to it the message I give you.'"
JONAH 3:1-2

God told Jonah again to go to Nineveh. Isn't it refreshing to know that when we blow it, God gives us second chances? Notice with me that God wasn't just giving Nineveh a second chance to repent and change, He was also giving Jonah a second chance to repent and change.

Jonah repented while he was slowly drowning in the fish, and now, an opportunity appeared for a chance to do something. As he went to Nineveh, we see God's love for the city. He didn't call them "those violent, awful, godless pagans," which they were; He called them "the great city."

As followers of Christ, we are called to care for the safety, the economy, and the housing of our city. God isn't just filled with love for the individual; He is filled with love for the whole city. And out of love for the whole city, there may be seasons when we will work with religiously different people for the good of our city.

When natural disasters occur in a city, like hurricanes and earthquakes, anyone who is willing to help in the recovery effort should be embraced because they are working for the good of the city. Followers of Jesus should especially embrace this opportunity. Working side by side in a common cause for the greater good of our city is a wonderful witness for Christ.

We are to be civic-minded and work hard to make our city the best it can be.

We know that this is not our ultimate home. Our ultimate home is Heaven. We are aliens and strangers while we are here on this earth; but while we are here, we work for Jesus.

Citizens of the kingdom of God should be the best citizens in the cities of this. A follower of Jesus is a citizen of both cities. We are concerned, active, and serving both cities.

We know that one day the city of God will come down to heal the rest of the cities on this earth. While we are still in this world, we don't work to accrue power — we serve. This is the heart of God, and this is how "The Gulf Coast Will Be Saved!"

TODAY'S PRAYER
Father, I thank You today that I am a citizen in the kingdom of Heaven and a citizen on this earth. Help me to be civic-minded and loving by serving both cities with Your power and grace.

■ ■ ■

Day 20

"Then the word of the Lord came to Jonah a second time: 'Go to the great city of Nineveh and proclaim to it the message I give you.'"
JONAH 3:1-2

Many historians believe that March 16th, 597 BC, was the date when Israel was conquered by the nation of Babylon. As a result, the remaining citizens were forced to abandon Israel and relocate to Babylon, often referred to as "The Babylonian Exile."

Upon arriving, the Israelites chose to live on the outskirts of the city and form their own community. They did not want to be polluted by the city, so they chose not to associate with them.

Through the prophet Jeremiah, God wrote them a letter and told them to not live on the outskirts of the city, but to go inside it.

"This is what the Lord Almighty, the God of Israel, says to all those I carried into exile from Jerusalem to Babylon: 'Build houses and settle down; plant gardens and eat what they produce. Marry and have sons and daughters; find wives for your sons and give your daughters in marriage, so that they too may have sons and daughters. Increase in number there; do not decrease. Also, seek the peace and prosperity of the city to which I have carried you into exile. Pray to the Lord for it, because if it prospers, you too will prosper.'"
JEREMIAH 29:4-7

The Jewish people were in Babylon by the will of God, in that He was bringing judgment on Judah for their generations of rebellion against Him.

In God's plan they would be in Babylon a long time, so it was best for them to settle in and make the best of their lives and families there. God wanted the Jewish people to multiply in Babylon, just as they multiplied in Egypt. Exile didn't mean that God forgot about them or wanted to destroy them.

God wanted them to do good in their communities and be a blessing to their Babylonian neighbors. Ultimately, God caused them to be in Babylon and wanted them to be a blessing where they were set. Not only that, He wanted them to pray for the very leaders that forced them to live there.

Prayer and good works of all sorts are ways to "seek the peace [shalom] of the city." Although prayer and random acts of kindness are good, they only bring temporary peace. Followers of Jesus know that the only peace that lasts is the peace that was given to us by Jesus Christ on the cross.

God was telling these people who had brought this judgment on themselves because of their rebellion, that their lives were still in His hands. He had appointed an end to their suffering, and it wouldn't be quick, but they wouldn't be there forever, either.

He told them that their exile from Israel was going to last for 70 years, and just as He gave them the bad news, He also gives us insight into God's heart for His kids. It is one of the most quoted Bible verses in the church world today.

> **"'For I know the plans I have for you,' declares the Lord, 'plans to prosper you and not to harm you, plans to give you hope and a future.'"**
> **JEREMIAH 29:11**

God knew His plans, but His people didn't. He reminded them of who He was and of His character. He thinks about us and has plans for us. His plan was to prosper them even after receiving His judgment. God has a future and a hope for His people even when we hurt under deserved discipline or judgment.

When we mess up and receive punishment, the devil tries to rob us of our sense of God's future and a hope for us. But God tells us that His plans for us are still to prosper and protect us. We haven't gone too far. He still loves us. And while we wait for the fulfillment of those plans, we serve, bless, and pray for those where He has presently placed us.

TODAY'S PRAYER
Father, thank You for where I live. Open my eyes for opportunities to serve and seek the prosperity of our city. Thank You that Your plans for me are good; and because of that, I choose to walk in the shalom of God today.

■ ■ ■

Day 21

**"Jonah obeyed the word of the Lord and went
to Nineveh. Now Nineveh was a very large city;
it took three days to go through it."**
JONAH 3:1-3

Nineveh was the capital of the Assyrian empire, which today
is the nation of Iraq. It was the greatest city that the world had
yet to see. It actually took three days to walk around it, and as a
result it was an impregnable fortress; no army was large enough
to stretch around the city.

Jonah knew all the facts and could not help but be incredibly
intimidated by them. However, what Jonah was about to learn
is that when God calls us into a new city or into new territory,
He has already prepared the ground ahead of time.

Historians say that right before Jonah came to Nineveh, they
had experienced a series of revolts, plagues, famines, and
eclipses. As a result of all of this, they were ready to hear. God
was opening their eyes and ears to hear what He needed to
tell them.

When God called our family to start Coastal Church in 2009,
we were at a place where we needed to hear every word about
what to do. Church planting was still very new at the time in
America, and to say that we were clueless about what to do
would be a gross understatement.

One day, I was praying, and I said, "God, if you really want me to
do this, I need to find a job and I need to find some people that

will actually come to our church." We were living temporarily in another city, but I came into town for a few hours to run some errands. Before I headed home, I thought, "I'm going to swing by the old baseball field and see what changes have been made." I thought I was feeling nostalgic, but I was actually being led by the spirit of God.

When I drove to the field, I saw my old coaching buddy, Joe "Hutch" Hutchins, watering the field. I got out and Hutch yelled out, "Rev! What are you doing in town, visiting your folks?" I said, "No, we are moving back here, and we are going to start a church." (He was the first person that I told about the church.)

Hutch smiled and said, "That's great, I will be your first member. And by the way, I need a JV coach; do you want a job?"

In one moment, two prayers were answered. I had a job offer, and the church had its first member before we ever had a service.

Today, on Coastal Church's Daphne campus, is *Joe Hutchins Stadium.* It is a beautiful baseball field named after our first member and an incredible reminder that when God calls us to a new place, He has already prepared the ground for us.

Be encouraged today that wherever God is leading you, He has already done the work ahead of time. The answers are there, the people are ready, and they are waiting to receive God's direction through you.

TODAY'S PRAYER

Father, thank You for preparing me for what You have for me. Thank You for going ahead of me and preparing the people and the place to receive Your direction.

■   ■   ■

Day 22

"Jonah began by going a day's journey into the city, proclaiming, 'Forty more days and Nineveh will be overthrown.' The Ninevites believed God."
JONAH 3:4

To Jonah's shock, the people didn't laugh at him or try to kill him. Instead, they did the opposite — they believed God. Jonah didn't believe that God could change Nineveh and didn't even want to.

We need to ask God to help us to see our city the way that He sees it. We must desire for our city to be changed. God wants us to believe that radical change is possible and that He can really make a difference in our lives.

In 2015, God led our church to begin to dream about doing something for the less fortunate in our county. We envisioned a center where we could do job training, feed the hungry, and house the homeless. We wanted to help people defeat lifelong addictions to drugs and alcohol, and we found a building where we could do it in Bay Minette, Alabama.

The building was right in the heart of town and had more than enough room to do everything. The price was spot on and we began to pursue it. Throughout the process, doors kept closing left and right. The owners waffled, and finally the county told us that they wouldn't approve the plans. We were heartbroken.

As I drove out of the town, I prayed, "God, we know that You're going to bring so much life and hope to this place. I can't believe that You wanted us to do all this work, for this to end this way. I guess now the best thing for this town would be a vibrant life-giving church."

I prayed for God to send someone to start a new work there, and almost immediately, I sensed the Holy Spirit say, "*Coastal Church needs to do it.*" I said, "Lord, I will prepare a plan, I just need You to prepare a person."

Within one year, God sent us Steve and Andrea Burton. We have a beautiful building on the highway that we own free and clear, and our Bay Minette campus has so much influence in their town. Every Friday night in the fall at the area high school football games, the parking lot workers, ticket takers, and concession stand servers are all from Coastal Church. They proudly wear their Coastal Church shirts as they serve and bless their community.

Bay Minette was ready for Coastal Church. They believed God, and they are changing the culture through serving their community. They are showing all of us what followers of Jesus know: that while we are alive, we are here for others.

TODAY'S PRAYER
Father, thank You for Your heart for revival.
Thank You for preparing my heart to receive what You
want to say to me and help me to see my city
the way that You see it.

■　■　■

Day 23

"A fast was proclaimed, and all of them, from
the greatest to the least, put on sackcloth. When
Jonah's warning reached the king of Nineveh,
he rose from his throne, took off his royal robes,
covered himself with sackcloth and sat down in the
dust. This is the proclamation he issued in Nineveh:
'By the decree of the king and his nobles: Do not let
people or animals, herds or flocks, taste anything;
do not let them eat or drink. But let people and
animals be covered with sackcloth. Let everyone
call urgently on God. Let them give up their evil ways
and their violence. Who knows? God may yet relent
and with compassion turn from his fierce anger
so that we will not perish.'"

JONAH 3:5-8

Not only did Nineveh believe in God, they repented to God.
The Hebrew word for "repent" is the word "Shub" which means
"to turn" and it is used four times in the span of two verses. If
repentance is anything, it is not business as usual. When
repentance comes, something has to change, and something has
to be different.

In their case, the people of Nineveh took off their normal
clothes and put on sackcloth, which was a thick coarse cloth,
normally made from goat's hair. Wearing it displayed the
rejection of earthly comforts and pleasures.

Wherever they were on the social spectrum, they all
participated. The rich and the poor wore sackcloth and ashes,

as did the influential and those who were viewed as socially insignificant. They even repented on behalf of their animals, dressing them as if the animals were in mourning for the dead.

In their repentance, they cried "mightily to God." They came to God with passion and seriousness about their sin, and their need for His mercy and forgiveness. They repented of their evil ways and their violence, because repentance means that we change our minds and turn from our previous sinful actions. When we truly turn to God, we turn away from the things that displease Him.

Their repentance brought them hope. They said, "Who can tell if God will turn and relent, and turn away from His fierce anger." Repentance has hope in the mercy and love of God. It hopes that God will relent and that the repentant people will not perish. Jonah effectively preached the message of repentance, because in the fish he modeled it. Being a repentant sinner didn't disqualify Jonah from preaching repentance; it made his preaching even more effective.

God did this in a place where only He could get the credit. Assyria was the greatest power in the world at the time and they were also the cruelest. God used a repentant sinner to begin a cultural revolution in the most powerful city on earth.

TODAY'S PRAYER
Father, I thank You that what You did in Nineveh, You want to do again here. May today I remain confident in Your ability to reach people no matter how bad things get in our culture.

■　■　■

Day 24

"When God saw what they did and how they turned from their evil ways, He relented and did not bring on them the destruction He had threatened."
JONAH 3:10

We don't obligate God to forgive us when we repent.

Repentance appeals to God's mercy, not His justice. God didn't forever withhold His judgment on Nineveh. He delayed it for 150 years. The book of Nahum later recorded it.

God called Jonah to Nineveh because He wanted to show Jonah "what is happening in Nineveh is affecting Me. It grieves Me; and Jonah, you need to be grieving too."

Jonah didn't do this, but Jesus did.

Jesus was riding into Jerusalem on the last week of His life. He knew He would suffer at the hands of the leaders and the mob of this city. But instead of being full of wrath or absorbed with self-pity, the book of Luke says:

"When he saw the city, he wept over it and said, 'If you, even you, had only known on this day what would bring you peace—but now it is hidden from your eyes. . .because you did not recognize the time of God's coming to you."
LUKE 19:41–42,44

The great Princeton theologian B. B. Warfield wrote an essay called "The Emotional Life of Our Lord." In it, he considered every recorded instance in the Gospels that described the emotions of Christ.

He reveals that by far the most typical statement of Jesus' emotional life was the phrase "He was moved with compassion."

"Moved with compassion" is a Greek phrase that literally means He was moved from the depths of His being.

Dr. Warfield concludes that the Bible records Jesus Christ weeping twenty times, for every one time that He laughs. Why? Isaiah prophesied that He would be "a man of sorrows."

This was not because He was depressed. No, He had enormous joy in the Holy Spirit and in His Father; and yet He grieved far more than He laughed because His compassion connects *Him* with *us*. In other words, our sadness makes Him sad, and our pain brings Him pain.

Here, God grieved over Nineveh, which means He was letting the evil of the city weigh on Him. He suffered because of their sin. Their repentance was a response to His mercy, and so is ours.

TODAY'S PRAYER
Father, thank You for Your compassion and mercy.
Thank You for connecting to us in our pain
because You feel it, too.

■ ■ ■

Day 25

"But to Jonah this seemed very wrong, and he became angry. He prayed to the Lord, 'Isn't this what I said, Lord, when I was still at home? That is what I tried to forestall by fleeing to Tarshish. I knew that you are a gracious and compassionate God, slow to anger and abounding in love, a God who relents from sending calamity.'"
JONAH 4:1-2

Jonah preached and Nineveh responded. They prayed, fasted, and committed to God a turning from evil and violent ways. God turned Jonah into a city changer, a world changer. He used Jonah to bring a culturally transforming revolution. This would be the climax of any preacher's career, but Jonah was angry about it.

In verse 2 we see this ongoing argument between God and Jonah. Jonah ran from Nineveh not because he was afraid of failure, but because he was afraid of success. Jonah was angry at God because he didn't like the Ninevite people. He wanted them to be destroyed. When he preached, "in 40 days Nineveh will be overthrown", he did so with glee. He enjoyed it. At the core of Jonah's frustration was racism. He didn't like the people.

At the beginning of the 20th century, many white Protestants in America feared that they were about to be outnumbered by the influx of uneducated people that were immigrating in large numbers. Although there was no science to prove it, there arose a popular thought that disease was mostly caused by these immigrants. People thought the possibility of these diseases being brought into our country would weaken and replace our population. Out of this fear, there arose a pseudo-science called eugenics.

With no scientific evidence, eugenics claimed that everything from poverty, prostitution, and physical and mental disabilities could be dismissed through sterilization. Criminals and the feeble-minded should be forbidden to leave offspring behind them.

Based on sloppy readings of Gregor Mendel's pea pods and Charles Darwin's theories, people concluded, "Many social ills are caused by the proliferation of the wrong sort of people; with eugenics, that could be neatly nipped in the bud."

The American Museum of Natural History hosted conferences about it; it was taught in schools; it was celebrated in exhibits at the World's Fair; and it was even preached in pulpits. Thirty-two states out of the forty-eight adopted eugenics laws. The whole bogus science of eugenics was fueled by racism and sexism. Eugenics set apart nationalities as different breeds.

As a result, the thirty-two states that adopted eugenics laws sterilized over 60,000 people without consent — mostly minorities and those with disabilities. Between 1997-2010, another 1,400 women in California prisons were forcibly sterilized.

Jonah's anger toward the Ninevites turning to God in repentance shows that when we possess the wrong view of people, it strips us of our humanity, and enables us to take away the humanity in others. It happened in Jonah's day, and it still happens in ours.

Followers of Jesus have been called to change how society views humanity. We believe that every person who has ever been born has the divine image of God inside of them and because of that, every person has inherent value. All people are precious to God.

TODAY'S PRAYER
Father, thank You for Your grace and compassion towards all people. Help me to see others the way You see them. Help me to serve others with the same love and grace You have shown me. Transform my wrong thinking, so that You can use me to lead others to You.

■　■　■

Day 26

> "But to Jonah this seemed very wrong, and he
> became angry. He prayed to the Lord, 'Isn't this
> what I said, Lord, when I was still at home? That is
> what I tried to forestall by fleeing to Tarshish. I knew
> that you are a gracious and compassionate God,
> slow to anger and abounding in love, a God who
> relents from sending calamity.'"
> **JONAH 4:1-2**

Jonah's faith in God was not as deep and fundamental to his life
as his race and his nationality. We see this when Jonah was on
the boat fleeing God.

> "Then the sailors said to each other, 'Come, let
> us cast lots to find out who is responsible for this
> calamity.' They cast lots and the lot fell on Jonah.
> So they asked him, 'Tell us, who is responsible for
> making all this trouble for us? What kind of work
> do you do? Where do you come from? What is your
> country? From what people are you?'"
> **JONAH 1:7-8**

> "He answered, 'I am a Hebrew
> and I worship the Lord, the God of heaven,
> who made the sea and the dry land.'"
> **JONAH 1:9**

Notice that Jonah was asked about his race last, but he answered
the race question first. "I am a Hebrew." He reversed the order
and put his race first. Jonah's ethnicity was the most significant

part of his identity. Jonah was too aligned politically and emotionally with the national interests of Israel.

Christians should be involved in politics. Avoiding politics is essentially casting a vote for evil. Christian involvement in politics is a good thing because we can use it as a way of loving our neighbors. A follower of Jesus works for the common good.

Being patriotic is also a good thing. It is a wonderful thing to love our homes and where we grew up. We will tend to feel less animosity toward our neighbors who are different when we have adoration for where we live.

On every college campus today any expression of national pride is very often seen as fascist and racist. We should reject anti-patriotism as another form of extremism too. People who see a healthy love for their country as toxic, also reject the high integrity and heroism that helped form the country that has provided them the opportunity to criticize it.

Jesus loved where He lived. He looked out over the city and wept over it because people and places were going to be destroyed.

Jonah's love for Israel was not like this. His patriotism had turned into blood lust. This was why he was so opposed to preaching to them to repent.

When loyalty to his people and loyalty to the word of God were in conflict, Jonah chose his people.

A truly devoted follower of Jesus places God's Word above feelings and prejudices. Obedience to God's Word is the highest value.

TODAY'S PRAYER

Thank you, Jesus, for showing us how to love our city. Help us to not allow pride to keep us from loving those You are sending us to. Keep us rooted in Your Word so that we don't allow our feelings and prejudices to hinder us from serving others.

■ ■ ■

Day 27

**"Now, Lord, take away my life, for it is better
for me to die than to live."**
JONAH 4:3

Jonah was looking forward to seeing the hammer fall on the Ninevites, and when it didn't happen, he was plunged into the depths of despair. Jonah was willing to walk away from his relationship with God because he didn't get his way.

Everyone must live for something in order for life to have any meaning. Jonah felt like he no longer had any meaning in life because he lost his God. The same thing can happen to us if we don't build our life on the Word of God.

We may sincerely believe that Jesus died for our sins, but we may find security in our careers, our financial worth, or our reputation. Professing Christians can be racists, greedy materialists, and addicted to beauty and pleasure. Or we can worry about everything and have constant anxiety, working ourselves into an early grave. Christians can have Jesus in their lives and still have a very *shallow identity*.

For example, the Gospels show us that one of Jesus' disciples named Peter followed Jesus and had a shallow identity. On the night Jesus was betrayed and arrested, He warned Peter about what was going to happen and Peter ignored Him.

**"Then Jesus told them, 'This very night
you will all fall away on account of me, for it
is written: 'I will strike the shepherd, and the sheep**

**of the flock will be scattered. But after I have risen,
I will go ahead of you into Galilee.' Peter
replied, 'Even if all fall away on account of you,
I never will.' 'Truly I tell you,' Jesus answered, 'this
very night, before the rooster crows, you will disown
me three times.' But Peter declared, 'Even if I have
to die with you, I will never disown you. And all the
other disciples said the same.'"**

MATTHEW 26:31-35

Peter's identity came from the fact that he was part of Jesus'
inner circle. Peter's identity was not rooted in Jesus' love for
him. Peter's identity was in his own commitment and love for
Jesus he thought he had achieved, but that love was going to
be tested.

**"Then they seized him and led him away,
bringing him into the high priest's house, and
Peter was following at a distance. And when they
had kindled a fire in the middle of the courtyard
and sat down together, Peter sat down among
them. Then a servant girl, seeing him as he sat
in the light and looking closely at him, said, 'This
man also was with him.' But he denied it, saying,
'Woman, I do not know him.' And a little later
someone else saw him and said, 'You also are
one of them.' But Peter said, 'Man, I am not.' And
after an interval of about an hour still another
insisted, saying, 'Certainly this man also was
with him, for he too is a Galilean.' But Peter said,
'Man, I do not know what you are talking about.'
And immediately, while he was still speaking, the
rooster crowed. And the Lord turned and looked**

at Peter. And Peter remembered the saying of the
Lord, how he had said to him, 'Before the rooster
crows today, you will deny me three times.'
And he went out and wept bitterly."
LUKE 22:54-62

Peter thought he was more courageous than the rest of the
group, but he turned out to be the biggest coward in the group.

When we have shallow identities, we become blind to who we
are. When the test comes, we fail.

It was very traumatic for Peter because he discovered he really
wasn't the person that he thought he was, and he almost didn't
recover from it. Jesus personally and publicly restored him
because his whole identity had been shattered.

TODAY'S PRAYER
Father, help me to find my identity in You and Your
Word. Help me to see with clear eyes the issues of my
heart, and to be quick to bring them into obedience
to You. Thank You for Your grace to choose to use me
despite my shortcomings. Thank You for forgiving us
through the sacrifice of Your son, Jesus.

■　■　■

Day 28

"But the Lord replied, 'Is it right for you to be angry?' Jonah had gone out and sat down at a place east of the city. There he made himself a shelter, sat in its shade and waited to see what would happen to the city.'"
JONAH 4:4-5

Jonah told God off and went to sit in a shelter. He waited and hoped God would change His mind and still smite the Ninevites. Jonah was about to discover that God is the ultimate teacher as He prepares a little object lesson just for Jonah. Just like God prepared a fish to swallow Jonah, He prepared a plant to comfort Jonah as he waited and hoped for Nineveh's destruction.

"Then the Lord God provided a leafy plant and made it grow up over Jonah to give shade for his head to ease his discomfort, and Jonah was very happy about the plant."
JONAH 4:6

Jonah was happy about the vine. This is the first time we see Jonah happy about anything. He was selfish and petty. His happiness was just as carnal as his anger because both were all about him.

"But at dawn the next day God provided a worm, which chewed the plant so that it withered. When the sun rose, God provided a scorching east wind, and the sun blazed on Jonah's head so that he grew

faint. He wanted to die, and said, 'It would be better for me to die than to live.' But God said to Jonah, 'Is it right for you to be angry about the plant?' 'It is,' he said. 'And I'm so angry I wish I were dead.'"
JONAH 4:7-10

Jonah was an angry man. He was angry because God brought repentance to the Ninevites, and then Jonah became angry again when he got hot.

The Hebrew word for "anger" means "to be hot." In other words, God let Jonah feel some of the heat. Jonah felt totally justified in his anger about his plant being gone and in his anger about God saving Nineveh.

When Jonah said he was angry enough to die, he was saying, "I have no security." Jonah, in a very short period, let the plant become an idol. And once the idol was gone, he wanted to die.

Jonah felt that there was nothing worth living for beyond his own self-image or comfort.

"But the Lord said, 'You have been concerned about this plant, though you did not tend it or make it grow. It sprang up overnight and died overnight.'"
JONAH 4:10

God showed Jonah how hypocritical he was. In essence, He told him, "You think you have a right to be mad about the plant, but you have no personal investment in this plant. You have no interest in this plant at all except for what the plant provides for you in the moment. You act like you care, but you don't. Your idolatry is turning on you and that is why you are so mad."

The plant was not the thing that Jonah was so mad about; Jonah was frustrated with life.

When we encounter people who have tremendous mood swings, we have to be careful not to internalize it. They aren't solely frustrated with their present situation. They just live a life of internal turmoil and this current occasion is the excuse they now have to freak out.

TODAY'S PRAYER
**Father, examine my heart and point out
any selfish ways in me. Help me to deal
with my anger and frustrations by bringing them
to You and surrendering my right to be right.
I don't want to live angry or moody like Jonah.
Thank You for teaching me through his example.
I surrender to Your will and Your way.**

■ ■ ■

Day 29

"And should I not have concern for the great city of Nineveh, in which there are more than a hundred and twenty thousand people who cannot tell their right hand from their left—and also many animals?"
JONAH 4:11

This is how the book of Jonah ends. God showed Jonah that he pitied a plant that came and went overnight, but didn't care about 120,000 people who had been here longer. Sometimes we forget that human beings are going to live forever somewhere. We have to give them the opportunity to choose where that will be.

When God said, "They don't know their right from their left", He was saying that they don't know the difference between good and bad. They didn't have the ability to make moral decisions yet.

The book of Jonah is a complex one. At the end of Chapter 2, it looked like Jonah was about to make the change. He repented in the belly of the fish and was willing to do whatever God wanted. He sounded so gracious. So what happened to him? Like many of us, Jonah needed to have multiple exposures to God's grace.

He was like the blind man in the Gospel of Mark who had multiple encounters with Jesus.

"Jesus took the blind man by the hand and led him outside the village. When he had spit on the man's eyes and put his hands on him, Jesus asked, 'Do you

**see anything?' He looked up and said, 'I see people;
they look like trees walking around.' Once more
Jesus put his hands on the man's eyes. Then his
eyes were opened, his sight was restored,
and he saw everything clearly."**
MARK 8:23–25.

It will take more than one encounter with God to see people the same way that God sees them. Experiences with disappointment and failure allow us to see our need for God's grace. To get God's love and Christ's grace down into the foundational layer of our identities is a process, and often a slow one.

Jonah 4:11 is the last verse in the book of Jonah. So what happened to Jonah? Was this a choose-your-own-adventure story here? Did Jonah ever get the message and change?

We can make a reasonable guess, that he did, in fact, change. How can we be sure? Jonah was so defiant. How can we know he changed? By asking ourselves this question: Who was the author of the story? Who wrote the book of Jonah?

The author of the book of Jonah was none other than Jonah himself. What kind of a man would let the world see how stupid he was?

A man who was now fully secure in God's love. A man who believed that you can be sinful and still be accepted. A man who knew that you can love God and still have a shallow identity. A man who found grace in the power of God.

And if God can change Jonah, He can change all of us and give us a new understanding of who He is.

TODAY'S PRAYER

Father, help me to find my identity in You and Your Word. Help me to see with clear eyes the issues of my heart, and to be quick to bring them into obedience to You. Thank You for Your grace to choose to use me despite my shortcomings. Thank You for forgiving us through the sacrifice of Your son, Jesus.

■　■　■